Heart to Heart

Velisa Oliver

WESTBOW·
PRESS
A DIVISION OF THOMAS NELSON
& ZONDERVAN

Scripture taken from the King James Version of the Bible.

Scripture taken from the Holy Bible, NEW INTERNATIONAL VERSION®. Copyright © 1973, 1978, 1984 by Biblica, Inc. All rights reserved worldwide. Used by permission. NEW INTERNATIONAL VERSION® and NIV® are registered trademarks of Biblica, Inc. Use of either trademark for the offering of goods or services requires the prior written consent of Biblica US, Inc.

WestBow Press books may be ordered through booksellers or by contacting:

WestBow Press
A Division of Thomas Nelson & Zondervan
1663 Liberty Drive
Bloomington, IN 47403
www.westbowpress.com
1 (866) 928-1240

Because of the dynamic nature of the Internet, any web addresses or links contained in this book may have changed since publication and may no longer be valid. The views expressed in this work are solely those of the author and do not necessarily reflect the views of the publisher, and the publisher hereby disclaims any responsibility for them.

Any people depicted in stock imagery provided by Thinkstock are models, and such images are being used for illustrative purposes only. Certain stock imagery © Thinkstock.

ISBN: 978-1-4908-7110-3 (sc)
ISBN: 978-1-4908-7111-0 (e)

Library of Congress Control Number: 2015902958

Print information available on the last page.

WestBow Press rev. date: 03/11/2015

Contents

Introduction

"Heart to Heart" is your inspirational book composed of heartfelt poems, for your quiet moments alone with God.

As you begin to read this book I pray that each of you will be inspired, encouraged and have hope for each day. I also pray that you will never give up no matter what situations you may face in life.

May God's spirit minister to your heart and enlighten you.

God Bless
Lisa

All Things Work Together

When you are to the point
That your back is against the wall
You've done everything possible
With no results at all

We know that in all things
God works for the good
Of those who love him

No weapon formed against you will prevail
Victory is on the way
Your testimony you will surely tell

Be sure to thank God that all is well

Amazing Grace

Lord thank you for your amazing grace
Without it I could not finish this race
Whenever I am in trouble
I call out to you
Without hesitation
You come to my rescue

Thank you for the joy and peace
You give to me, because of your spirit
I know that I am free

Your grace is sufficient in every way
When I look back over my life
I see it was you who carried me
From day to day

Angels

There are angels watching over us
Each and every day
Our Father in Heaven
Has assigned them to us
To protect along the way

These angels we cannot see
Neither can we hear
Anytime we are in danger
We know they are near

Some men wear them as pendants
Upon a shirt or tie
Just know when you're in harm's way
Your assigned angel is standing by

Another Day

Each morning at the sound of my alarm
Not ready to get out of bed just yet
Because it's nice and warm

I give thanks to the Lord for another day
Praying for divine protection along the way

I arrive to work ready for what I must face
So much going on I ask you Father for your grace

Now the day has come to an end
I am headed for home
Then it starts all over again

Awesome Ruler

Jesus, Jesus
You are the King
Who reigns over all

You are an awesome ruler
You give me the strength
To stand when I feel
As though I am about to fall

You oh Lord are faithful
And loyal in all that you do
Each morning we are undeserving
But you give us mercies brand new

Bless Me

Dear God please hear my prayer
As I come to you my heart is in despair
So many burdens have fallen upon me
So once again here I am on bended knee

Lord I need you to bless me
Like only you can
No one else can fix it
No human man

I know you are a God
Who will not fail
No weapon formed against me
Will ever prevail

So by faith I believe
You have worked things out
And will surely
Bless me without a doubt

Believe

Believe that you can do all things
Through Christ if his spirit lives
On the inside of you

He has given you the power
And authority concerning
Situations in your life
Nothing will be impossible to do

With Christ you will not fail
Only believe within your heart
God's purpose and plan
For your life will prevail

Brighter Day

Yesterday is gone
Today is brand new
Praying for the storm clouds
To no longer be
A part of my view

Looking forward to
A brighter day
Trouble don't last always
Soon these storm clouds
Will have to pass away

The sun will come out to shine once more
Whenever God closes a window
He has an open door

Daily Prayer

Thank you Lord for waking me this day
Seeing me safely as I go on my way

My every thought I will surrender to you
Let my actions be pleasing in all that I do

Thank you for new mercies
Thank you for your grace
Awakening me to
A beautiful sunshine
Upon my face

Destiny

When God created man
He must have had a purpose in mind
I do believe that we all have a destiny to fulfill
It's just a matter of time

When Destiny calls out your name
If you decide to answer
Let your motives be right
Don't labor in vain

God will have his hand upon you
The gifts he has given will start to manifest
Through your life for the purpose he has called you to

Don't be afraid to step out in faith and give it a try
God does not show you everything from the beginning
And there's a reason why

Don't Look Back

When you know what Jesus
Has called you to do
Take your place and
Run your race
Where ever
He is leading you

Keep your eyes
Looking straight ahead
Remember not to look back
The past is already dead

At every turn he will always be there
To watch over you with
His tender loving care

Dream

It's ok for a person to dream
No matter how big or small
Or even ridiculous it may seem

Go ahead and dream
It is all for a reason
God put it in your heart
To bring it to pass at
The right time and season

Don't listen to the negative talk
Of the people around you
And what they have to say

You don't need anyone's approval
Because guess what
They're going to talk any way

So go ahead and dream
Put it in God's hands
When it comes to pass
That's when you know
It was all a part of his plan

Every Step

Lord thank you for bringing
Me through so much

Forever you are present with me
Leading the way with
Your gentle touch

Every step that I take
You are right by my side
When I can't see my way clear
My eyes you will open wide

Thank you for leading my path
From day to day
Trusting your guidance
With every step that I take

Faith

What is this thing called faith
What does it mean?

It is the substance of things hoped for
The evidence of things not seen

Step out on faith and do what God
Is telling you to do

For with faith nothing will be impossible for you

When the going gets tough
You must be willing to fight
Remember you are walking
By faith and not by sight

Family Matters

How did marriage first come to be?
It started out with a man called
Adam and a woman named Eve

God said that it was not good
For man to be alone
He was surely right
Because women take
Care of the home

Children are born
To bring them much joy
What will it be?
A girl or a boy

The husband is to provide for his mate
To be faithful at all times to his wife
Because adultery is something that
God surely will not tolerate

Follow Your Heart

When God speaks
He speaks to the heart of man
You must be quiet and still
To hear his voice
So that you will understand

God will never steer you
Any place wrong
He will give you clues along the way

To keep you on the path
Where ever you belong

Next time you hear a still small voice
Follow your heart and ask God
For the right decision
Before you make a choice

God's Favor

Only you God can show me your favor
When my life pleases you
That is why I try my best
To be a faithful servant
In all that I do

Those who find you find life
And receive your favor indeed
For you Lord God will do
Above and beyond
To meet my every need

Lord you bless the righteous
You surround them
With your favor as a shield

For that I say thank you
To you my spirit I will yield

God has the Final Say

When the challenges of life come your way
And it seems like all hope is gone
Stand still and wait for God
He will bring deliverance
He will help you to be strong

Don't worry he knows everything
That you will have to go through
You are never alone
God is still in control upon his throne
With his hand he will carry you

Continue to pray throughout the day
Just know in your heart
God always has the final say

God Is Able

In life things don't always go according to plan
There may be major setbacks
Some you may not understand

The dreams you had
May have been put on hold
However don't let it stop you
From reaching your goal

Keep the faith move straight ahead
Even when you feel like you're
Hanging on barely by a thread

Just know that our God is able
Any day he can turn the table

God the Creator

It started with a word when God spoke let there be light
He gives us the sun for daytime
The moon for the darkness at night

He created the oceans and the rivers
That surrounds our land
He is almighty and powerful
And holds the world in his hand

He regulates both the times and the seasons
So when the leaves on a tree begin to change color
It's all for a reason

We see his wonderful creation
Before our very eyes
The high mountains
The beautiful waterfalls
Caterpillars that turn into butterflies

God is Alpha and Omega
The beginning and the end
He is so full of wisdom that
No human mind can comprehend

God the Provider

Heavenly Father you will meet and supply
my every need
Whether physical, spiritual or emotional
No matter whatever it may be

When the budget is low and the money is tight
I don't have to worry
Because I know you will make it alright

When I don't know where the next meal will come from
To put food on the table
Somehow you will make a way
You are God and you are more than able

Grateful

Heavenly Father I am grateful
For all that you have done for me
I know just how blessed I am
By looking around every day at what I see

People are sleeping
Out on the streets
They have no place to stay
While others are walking
With their bare feet
Mostly throughout the day

Lord I am so grateful
That I have a place to rest
And lay my head
When so many people
Go to sleep at night without
Even a bed

Thank you for the food each day
You put on my table
So anytime I can bless others
It is because of you
That I am able

Great Is Thy Faithfulness

Our Father who is in heaven
Great is thy faithfulness

God you are so faithful in all your ways
When I look back over my life
It was you who provided for me
Many of my days

When all of my bills became due
Sometimes not knowing
How they would get paid
You always came through

I just want to say thank you Lord
For all that you do
By expressing the love
I have in my heart
That is all for you

Hallelujah

Hallelujah to our Lord and King
Who is seated at the right hand
Of the Father and whose praises
I daily sing

Thank you Jesus for saving me
If it was not for you
Who knows where would I be?

How I love to worship and praise your holy name
From the rising of the sun to the going down of the same

Only you oh Lord are worthy of the honor
For all that you have done
There is no one before or after you
No one else to come

Heaven

Father I can't wait to get to Heaven
So I may see your face
To meet my Lord and Savior
To hear him speak well done
My faithful servant
You have finished your race

To have my own mansion
Is better than any house
I ever occupied on earth
To walk the streets of gold
For all that it's worth

To see all of my love ones
Who will be waiting there for me
To enter into the pearly gates
Of heaven what a joy it will be

Help Is On the Way

In this life that we live
There will be your ups and downs
Sometimes we have to pretend
Like everything is ok and smile
Instead of wearing a frown

It is often said that trials
Come to make you strong
We are being tried in the fire
But at times the fire seems way too long

If we can learn to trust in the Lord
Before the trouble comes our way
Then the load we carry may be a little lighter
At the end of the day

When you wake up each morning
Don't forget to pray
Before you go to sleep at night
Know that help is on the way

Hope for Tomorrow

If your today is cloudy and filled with sorrow
Whatever the challenge may be
Just know there is hope for tomorrow

Don't stress and worry
Pray and leave in God's hands

Before you know it
He will work things out for you
In such a way that
You could not begin to understand

Look back in the past
See how he has brought you through
Over and over again

This will not be his first time
It will surely not be the end

I Am

God you are the great I Am
What does that mean to me?

The answer to the question is
That you are whatever it is I need
I know that you will be

You are my deliverer when I am in trouble
I call on your precious name
And you are there on the double

When I am thirsty
You are the well
That will never run dry

When I feel sad and began to cry
I find comfort in your presence
You wipe away the tears from my eyes

I Will Sing

I will sing to the Lord for he has been good to me
I was called out of darkness
Set on the path to my destiny

I will worship him with songs from my heart
Nothing could ever keep us apart

I will praise and honor his holy name
Since Jesus came into my life
I will never ever be the same

No rocks will ever cry out for me
I will sing to the Lord
Now and for eternity

Jesus

God our Father who loved us so
That he gave his only son
Just know with confidence
That any battle you face
The victory is already won

They nailed his hands to the cross
At that point it seemed that all hope was loss
With his arms stretched out wide
His mother present and spectators watching
He hung his head and died

They took him off the cross and laid him in a tomb
This man they called Jesus had come from Mary's womb
The disciples thought they would never see Jesus again
But he rolled away the stone and
showed himself once more
So they knew it was not the end

Because of his resurrection we have hope for each day
Knowing that a man called Jesus is leading us
And will always make a way

Jesus the Redeemer

Thank you Jesus for the blood that you shed
It's now by your spirit I am being led

Jesus the Redeemer that's who you are to me
It started way back on Calvary
Because of you I am no longer lost
The victory is mine due to the cross

You gave your life in my place
You took on my sins
Because of your grace

Because of the love you had for me
Whom The Son sets free is free indeed

Joy

Unspeakable joy that is what Jesus
Gives down in my soul
I would not trade it for anything
In this world no silver or gold

Joy, that's what I have even when
The storm clouds in life
Are hanging over my head
I can still smile and be happy
When it looks like I should
Be sad instead

Don't let the problems in life get to you
Choose to have unspeakable joy

No matter what's going on
You can still be happy
In spite of whatever
You are going through

Letter to Jesus

Lord there is so much I want to say
I do not even know where to start
Let me begin by expressing
All of the love that I have
Deep within my heart

Thank you for your life and your precious blood
It was because of the cross and your sacrifice
You took my place so I would not have to pay the price

I can't wait to see you face to face
To have you wrap your arms around me
To feel your warm embrace

I want to say thank you Jesus for taking me by the hand
In the tough times when
I didn't think I was going to make it
You were my rock and gave me the strength to stand

Light of the World

Jesus is the Light of the World
Shining bright for all to see
Every man, women, boy and girl

Your light overpowers darkness in every way
It is your light that will make a difference
In our day to day

Jesus is the light that will never go dim
To those who make the faithful choice
Be sure to put your trust in him

Listen

Can you hear the Voice of God?
What he wants to say
Open up your heart to him
Let him lead the way

He wants to embrace you
With an everlasting love
To fill you with his presence
That can only come from above

God wants to have a relationship
That is like no other
He will stick closer to you
Than any friend, sister or brother

So open up your heart
If you hear him knocking at the door
He will come in to abide with you
Now and forever more

Lord Prepare Me

Lord prepare me for the work
That you have called me to
Whatever your will is
That is what I want to do

Please give me provision
And meet my every need
Along the way
Help me in my struggles day to day

Give me the courage to always stand
For what is good
And do what is right

Lord teach me your ways
That I may be pleasing in your sight

Lord You're Mighty

Lord you are a mighty God
You are awesome in all that you do
Your ways are so beyond us
There is no one else like you

You alone Lord are worthy of all the praise that I give
It is because of what you did for me on the cross
This Christian life is what I choose to live

In your perfect will is where I want to be
To stay under your protection
To receive all of the blessings
You have in store for me

Love

God loved us so that he gave his only son
Why then can't we love one another as we should?
It is not to be based on a person's race
Or whether you are bad or good

Love cost nothing
It was given to us for free
You can't pay cash or charge it
There is no annual fee

Love has no color
Black, white, yellow or green
It is being kind to everyone
And should never be mean

Never Give Up

When it seems as though
Life has gotten the best of you
You are walking around stressed
And don't know what to do

Never give up
Know that God has a plan
He holds you in the palm
Of his very own hand

He is watching over you
With his very eye
He sees every tear
That you may ever cry

Weeping may endure for a night
Joy will come with the morning light

Never Too Late To Get It Right

It is never too late
For you to get it right
God is always waiting to hear from you
Whether it is day or night

You can come to him
Just as you are
You don't have to be perfect
Because no one is
Nearby or far

God can take the broken pieces
From your life and put them together again
He will never leave or forsake you
Just know he will be there
With you till the very end

Obedience

It is better to obey God rather than man
When he ask you to do something
Do not question it, even if you don't understand

Do it by faith, everything God has said
Sometimes it will make no sense
When you begin to think about it within your head
His thoughts and his ways are so beyond our imagination
Whatever he ask you to do it's all for a purpose
So do it without hesitation

Oh Happy Day

It was such a happy day
When Jesus came to rescue me
Once I was blinded by darkness
Now my eyes are open to see

He brought me out
Into his kingdom of light
Gave me his spirit that would
Teach me to pray
Worship and fight

Jesus can turn your life
Completely around
Place your feet on solid ground

Oh what a happy day
My Savior is leading me
All the way

Order My Steps

Lord as I head out of the door on my way
I ask that you will lead and guide
Every step for today

Not only for today
Also for my path in life
That you will give me clear directions
When to turn left
Or when to make a right

Lord please keep my feet planted on solid ground
I need you to lead and guide my spirit daily
That I will never be turned around

I want to reach the place of destination
That you have prepared for me
I am going to run on and
See what the end result will be

Praise Is What I Do

Praise is what I have learned to do
No matter what
It is I am going through

Whether times are good or bad
Doesn't matter if I am happy or sad

Lord I will bless your holy name
When I do I know that my situation
Will not remain the same

You deserve all honor and glory
When this trial is over
I will gladly tell my story

Prince of Peace

Thank you Lord for giving your peace to me
During the time of my storms
You calm the raging sea

The peace that you give
Some just can't understand
It is clear to those who truly know you
For the ones who have taken your hand

When I lay my head down to rest at night
I know that everything will be all right

Jesus you know how to fix things so well
Just like you did for Paul
While locked up in a cell
You sent the angels down and
Released him from jail

Search Me Lord

Search my heart Dear Lord
I want my motives to be right
In everything that I do

My life is about serving others
And of course pleasing you

I look for nothing in return
Only to be a blessing to your kingdom
That is what my heart yearns

Take away everything
That is not like you
Cleanse and wash me
Giving me the Mind of Christ
That has been renewed

Seasons

Seasons come and seasons go
Like the shifting of the wind
You feel it but never
See where it blows

There is a time and season
For everything
A time to be sad
A time to be happy
A time to rejoice and sing

Life is always changing
It never stays the same
No matter if you have nothing
Or whether you have riches
Fortune and fame

Strength

Thank you Jesus that you gave
Your life for me way back on Calvary

Because of unconditional love
And your precious blood
I have hope for each new day

Hope for a brighter tomorrow
Even when my days
Are filled with sorrow

I know that you are walking
With me hand in hand
So whatever I face daily
You will give me the strength to stand

The Best is Yet to Come

Your future shall be greater than your past
Whatever troubles you're having now
Remember it's only temporary
They are not going to last

God has given provision
To meet all of your needs
Your harvest will come
Just always sow good seed

Just trust in him and believe
Your answer is on the way
Don't give up
By faith you shall receive

The Call

God has saved us and called us to a holy life
That we may live in peace with one another
Without jealousy and strife

It does not matter who you are
God can use anyone whether
Living near or far

It is not because of anything we have done
But because of his own purpose and grace

So if you hear his voice calling you
Be sure to answer and begin to seek
His face

Therefore make every effort to confirm
Your calling and election
And while serving God
Try to do it with perfection

The Cost

It cost Jesus his life upon the cross
He did it for me and he did it for you

So then what are you willing to give up?
In return if he asked
What would you do?

It would not come to the point of death
That is not how it will be
You may have to give up
A few pleasures in life

Surrender your heart to him
And let him use you accordingly

Before you answer the call
Consider the price you may have to pay
I can tell you for sure it will be worth the investment

To follow Jesus and receive his blessings
And provision for your life
From day to day

The Cross

Upon the cross my Savior died
Jesus gave his life and was crucified
They judged him so harshly
But he just let it be
They held him prisoner
And set the guilty man free

They whipped and they beat him
Until he bled all over the place
He was scarred and bruised
You could barely recognize his face

Jesus carried his cross all the way to Calvary
He didn't give up because it was for you and me

He looked up toward the heavens and said
Father forgive them for they know not what they do

So please remember his suffering
That he gave his life for you

The Gifts

The gifts that you gave to man
Are for your purpose and your glory
They are for honoring you
To advance the kingdom
To even share our story

The gifts you give to us
You will not take them back
Even though we mess up at times
We get ourselves off track

Thank you for the gifts
You have given to me
I will do my best
Above the rest
To use all of my gifts wisely

The Great Shepherd

A Great Shepherd is one who watches over his sheep
He leads them through green pastures
Provides water to drink and food for them to eat

The sheep know the shepherds voice
They listen to him and will not follow
A stranger and that is by their own choice

He will not let anyone come
To steal them away
If one happens to wander off
He will go in search of him
To bring back the very same day

The Perfect Time

Lord I am trying to wait patiently
On the answer from my prayer
That you will give to me

You may not answer the way
I think you should
But you know what's best
And will only do
What is for my good

However you choose to answer
That would be just fine
I know that you will show
It will be at the perfect time

The Potter's Wheel

To be on the potter's wheel
Does not always feel good
God is shaping and molding
You just as he should

He is the Potter
We are the clay within his hands
He takes away and adds to us
Just as much as he can

Stay on the potter's wheel
Until God is through molding you

When his work is all finished
You will be just like brand new

The Promise Keeper

Has God ever made you a promise?
And you're still waiting for it
To come true

Don't give up hope
Waiting on the promise
He will surely bring
It to pass for you

God is not a man that he should lie
Or change his mind
For the promise he made to you
Is for an appointed time

He speaks and then he acts
God is not like mankind
He will not take his promise back

The Unsaved

It is time for people to wake up
Take a look around at the world
We are living in today

God said it is not his will
That any man should perish
But turn from his wicked ways

Jesus is the way, the truth and the light
So many are walking in darkness
Therefore they have no sight

God says to come, humble yourselves and pray
He wants for you to seek his face

We serve a God that is full of mercy
And has amazing grace

He said that he will hear from Heaven
He will forgive your every sin

It's not too late for you to start now
He can give you new life within

The Vine and The Branch

Jesus you are the vine
And we are the branches
Connected to you just like a tree

If we are to bear fruit
We must remain in you
That is the way it has to be

Apart from you
We can do nothing
That is what your word has to say

If anyone does not remain in you
He is like a branch that withers
Such branches are picked up
And thrown away

To Know God

To know our Father
Is a beautiful thing
To be in a relationship
With him makes my heart sing

God is concerned about all
That concerns me
I can enter into his door
Without needing a key

He watches over me
While I'm awake or sleep
He gives me protection
Seven days a week

Trusting God

When life around you seems
To be tumbling down
You cry out to God but it looks like
He is nowhere to be found
God is teaching you to trust in him

I know it is hard because
You can't see a way out
God is faithful and he will bring
You deliverance without a doubt

When you have done
All the crying that you can do
Just know at the end of the day
The favor of God
Will open up a door for you

Twinkling of a Star

Twinkle, twinkling of a star
Father your creation is amazing
How marvelous you are

You created the stars to beam
At night above in the sky
Placed them perfectly to be seen
By the eye

Your beautiful works need no correction
In all that you do it is to perfection

Thanks for the moon and stars at night
Even if the streets lights are not working
The stars will still be shinning bright

Use Me

Dear Jesus I pray that you will use me
Every day
To make a difference in this world
To be a blessing anyway I can for
Any man, woman, boy or girl

Something as simple as putting shoes
On someone's bare feet or buying
A meal for a hungry person
Who otherwise would not have food to eat

If everyone will just open up
Their hearts and do whatever they can

Our world could be so much better
By showing love and kindness
Towards our fellow man

Victory

Victory, Victory that is what we proclaim
There is always victory in Jesus name

When the enemy comes against you to attack
Remember there are scriptures
That you must use to fight him back

You are soldiers in the army of God
So take up your spiritual weapons
And place them in your hand

God has not given you a spirit of fear
So fear nothing
Not even man

Walk With Me Lord

Walk with me Lord
I need you every day
To be by my side

When I am not sure which way to go
I know that you will give me directions
You will be my guide

You will hold me by the hand
When I hear your voice
I will follow your every command

From your path I will not stray
Never to be led by another
No one else can take me away

CPSIA information can be obtained
at www.ICGtesting.com
Printed in the USA
FSOW01n0117080515
6986FS